WEIRD-BUT-TRUE FACTS ABOUT EARTH

BY LAUREN COSS • ILLUSTRATED BY KATHLEEN PETELINSEK

Published by The Child's World®
1980 Lookout Drive • Mankato, MN 56003-1705
800-599-READ • www.childsworld.com

Acknowledgments
The Child's World®: Mary Berendes, Publishing Director
Red Line Editorial: Editorial direction
The Design Lab: Design
Amnet: Production

ISBN 9781614734130
LCCN 2012946520

Printed in the United States of America
Mankato, MN
November, 2012
PA02143

About the Author

Lauren Coss is a writer and editor who lives in Saint Paul, Minnesota. She loves learning new facts about the planet she lives on.

About the Illustrator

Kathleen Petelinsek loves to draw and paint. She lives next to a lake in southern Minnesota with her husband, Dale; two daughters, Leah and Anna; two dogs, Gary and Rex; and her fluffy cat, Emma.

TABLE OF CONTENTS

INTRODUCTION

The planet Earth is an amazing place! There is never a dull moment on the third planet from the sun. Volcanoes erupt, earthquakes rock the surface, and the continents shift around thanks to **tectonic plates**. Get ready to learn more about the planet we call home. The facts in this book may seem out of this world, but remember, they are all true!

ROCKIN' AND ROLLIN'

The Earth's tectonic plates move about as fast as your fingernails grow.

That is about 2 inches (5 cm) a year.

In Death Valley, California, some rocks are on the run.

Scientists have found tracks behind rocks in a dry lake bed showing they have moved as fast as a person walks. Some of these rocks are more than 700 pounds (300 kg). No one has ever seen these rocks in motion.

Earth's orbit is slowing down.

The planet turns approximately 2 milliseconds slower every 100 years.

One of the biggest earthquakes in the United States was in the Midwest.

Beginning in December 1811, a series of giant earthquakes rocked the area around New Madrid, Missouri. The quakes were strong enough to ring church bells in Boston, Massachusetts. They even caused the Mississippi River to appear to flow backwards for a time.

The largest rock on Earth can be seen from almost 100 miles (160 km) away.

Mount Augustus in the Australian Outback is 2,352 feet (717 m) high. Australia's original inhabitants called it Burringurrah.

MOUNT AUGUSTUS
100 MILES
(160 KILOMETERS)

WELCOME TO THE AUSTRALIAN OUTBACK

Mammoth Cave in Kentucky is the longest known cave system on Earth.

It stretches for more than 390 miles (627 km), and that's just what has already been explored. Some scientists believe Mammoth Cave may be more than 600 miles (1,000 km) long. That's about the distance from Boston, Massachusetts, to Cleveland, Ohio!

Animals can predict earthquakes.

Animals from frogs to dogs can sense the beginning of an earthquake before humans feel any shaking. Many stories tell of animals sensing quakes days or weeks in advance, but these stories have not been proven by science.

FROM POLE TO POLE

Antarctica looks twice as big in the winter as it does in the summer.

In the winter, sea ice forms around the continent making it appear double in size.

If you want to lose weight, head to the equator.

A person who weighs 150.8 pounds (68.4 kg) at the North Pole weighs only 150 pounds (68 kg) at the equator. Because the pull of gravity is stronger at the poles, objects weigh less the farther away they are from them.

The static on your radio might be caused by the aurora borealis.

Known as the northern or southern lights, this **phenomenon** can be seen in both hemispheres. It occurs when solar radiation hits the Earth's magnetic field. This creates brightly colored lights that flicker across the sky, especially near the north and south poles. The radiation can interfere with radio and satellite communications.

There is no solid land under the North Pole, only sea ice.

More than 68 percent of Earth's fresh water is locked up in permanent ice, including the ice caps and glaciers.

Icebergs can float really far south.

In 1926, an iceberg was spotted in Bermuda.

Antarctica is the best place to go meteorite hunting.

The icy continent has a snowy landscape and little vegetation, so meteorites are easy to spot on the ground. More meteorites have been found in Antarctica than anywhere else in the world.

There are two north poles and two south poles.

One is the pole that Earth's **meridians** run through. The other is the magnetic pole, where a compass needle points.

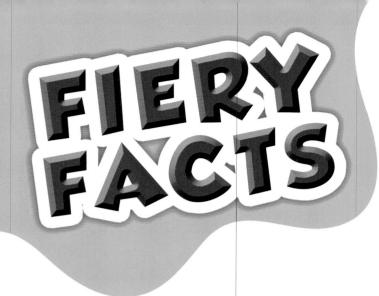

FIERY FACTS

The eruption of Krakatoa volcano in Indonesia was heard across 10 percent of the globe.

The eruption in 1883 made the loudest sound in recorded history. It was so violent it literally blew Krakatoa off the face of the Earth. Now, a new volcano is growing in its place.

Yellowstone National Park is actually a gigantic volcano.

It is still active, although the most recent eruption was before humans existed. Scientists believe the eruption threw ash all the way to the Gulf of Mexico.

WELCOME TO YELLOWSTONE

The largest meteorite impact in recorded history flattened trees for 800 square miles (2,100 sq km).

The giant space rock struck Tunguska, Siberia, in 1908. Scientists have not found the meteorite, and the event is not fully explained.

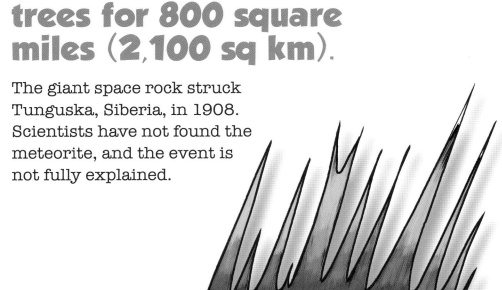

North America's youngest volcano was born in 1943.

Parícutin volcano began as a steaming mound in a farmer's field in Mexico. Within a year, it was more than 1,000 feet (330 m) high and still growing. It erupted until 1952 and now stands more than 10,400 feet (3,170 m) high.

Mount Kilimanjaro is actually a volcano.

It is one of the highest volcanoes in the world, though it is no longer active. Its peak is more than 3.5 miles (5.9 km) high. It has year-round snow even though it is very close to the equator.

One type of rock can float.

Pumice stone is created from the ash spewed out by a volcano. It is full of tiny air bubbles that make it so lightweight it can float on water.

The Earth's core is hotter than the sun.

Scientists believe the core may be as hot as 13,000 degrees Fahrenheit (7,000°C). The surface of the sun is thought to be approximately 10,000 degrees Fahrenheit (6,500°C).

Some trees need fire to reproduce.

Lodepole pinecones can only release their seeds during a forest fire. Fire is a natural and important part of many habitats.

WATER WONDERS

Sometimes waves glow electric blue.

In some places, tiny animals called plankton shine like fireflies, which makes the ocean appear to be glowing.

The deepest place on Earth is much deeper than the highest place on Earth.

The Marianas Trench in the Pacific Ocean is the deepest place on Earth. If you put Mount Everest at the bottom of the trench, you would have more than 1 mile (1.6 km) of water above the mountain's summit.

There is one sea that has no coast.

Several ocean currents border the Sargasso Sea, located near Bermuda in the Atlantic Ocean. The currents create a large area of still water full of floating seaweed. It is the only sea on Earth that is defined by ocean currents rather than a land border.

Angel Falls is as tall as a 300-story building.

This mighty waterfall in Venezuela falls 3,212 feet (979 m), making it the tallest waterfall on Earth.

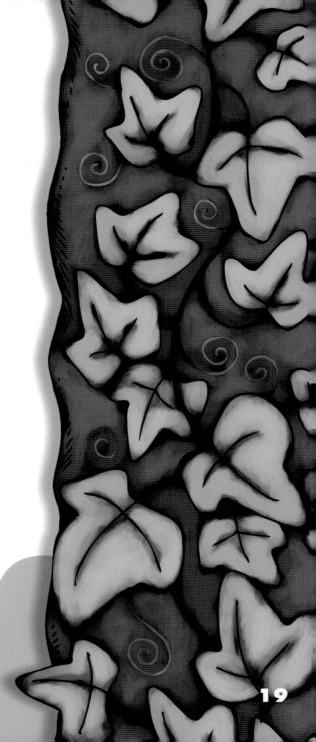

19

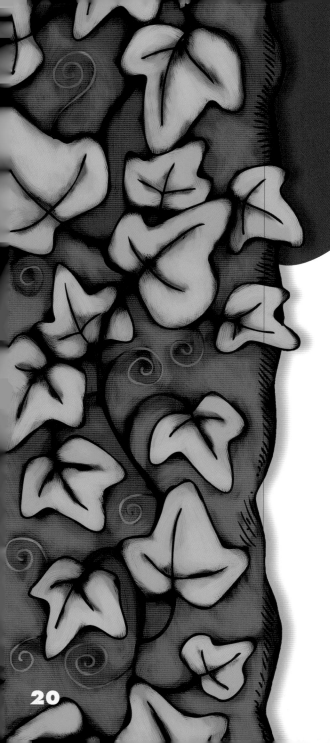

There is enough water in the Great Lakes to cover the United States to a depth of nearly 10 feet (3 m).

Lake Baikal in Russia is almost 1 mile (1.6 km) deep.

The lake holds 20 percent of the Earth's unfrozen fresh water. It is the deepest and the oldest lake in the world.

The Great Barrier Reef can be seen from space.

It is the only living thing that can be seen from so far away. The reef is more than 1,200 miles (2,000 km) long. It runs off the coast of Australia.

The world's tallest geyser reaches more than 30 stories high.

Steamboat Geyser in Yellowstone National Park has been known to spray water more than 300 feet (91 m) high. Its eruptions can last more than 40 minutes.

Humans have explored less than 5 percent of the ocean.

PLANT AND TREE TIDBITS

Some plants eat meat.

The nepenthes plant, or pitcher plant, makes a tasty juice that animals try to drink. When an animal, such as a small lizard, enters the plant's cupped leaves, it cannot get out. The plant then gets nutrients from the trapped animal.

The yew tree is one of Earth's most toxic plants.

Every part of the tree is poisonous except its red berries. It is planted in many graveyards across the United Kingdom and symbolizes death and the afterlife.

Some tree sap can erode car paint.

The manchineel tree of the Caribbean is so poisonous it can cause lung problems in people who simply inhale its smoke or sawdust. The sap is so **toxic** it can ruin the paint on a car parked underneath the tree. The sap also causes human skin to blister.

There are no black flowers.

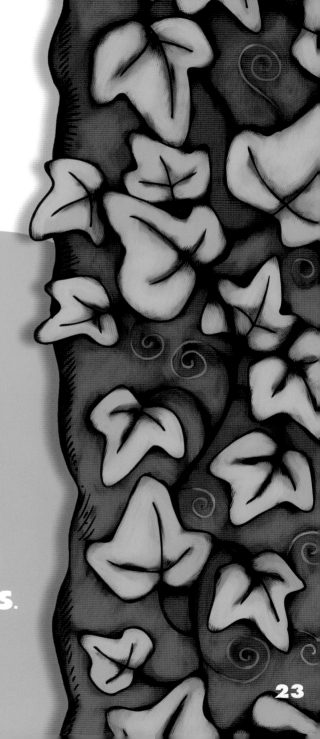

Each day, a single oak tree can drink enough water to fill seven bathtubs.

Lily pads are not just for frogs anymore. Some can support the weight of a child.

Called water platters, these South American freshwater plants can be as big as 6 feet (1.8 m) across.

No matter how high a tree grows, a birdhouse in it won't move.

Trees grow up from the top, so the birdhouse will always be the same distance from the ground.

Some willow trees can communicate with each other.

Scientists have found that when insects attack a willow, the tree produces a chemical that other trees can detect. When neighboring trees get this signal, they change the chemical makeup of their leaves to keep the bugs away.

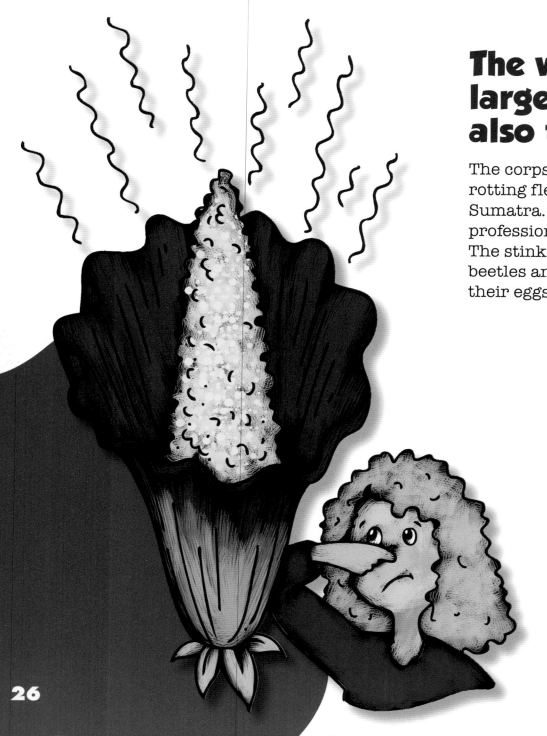

The world's largest flower is also the smelliest.

The corpse flower smells like rotting flesh. It is native to Sumatra. It can be taller than a professional basketball player. The stink attracts insects such as beetles and flies that like to lay their eggs in dead animals.

Want to breathe easy? Plant a tree!

One adult tree can remove 48 pounds (21 kg) of pollution from the atmosphere each year. One tree can also put enough oxygen back in the atmosphere to support two humans for a year.

There are 7,500 kinds of apples.

Apples originated in central Asia. The crabapple is the only native North American apple.

A bushel of corn, made into corn syrup, can flavor 400 cans of soda.

Watching bamboo grow is anything but boring.

A bamboo plant can grow more than 2 inches (5.1 cm) an hour. At this rate, it's one of the fastest-growing plants on Earth.

The world's oldest tree was accidentally cut down in 1964.

A scientist cut down the Utah bristlecone pine for research. After counting the tree's rings, the scientist realized the tree was 4,900 years old. Today, the oldest tree is a 4,765-year-old bristlecone pine that lives in California.

A tree about twice as tall as the Statue of Liberty lives in a California forest.

This redwood tree stretches nearly 380 feet (116 m) high and is the tallest known tree on the planet. It is nicknamed "Hyperion."

Oak trees are late bloomers.

An oak can reach 50 years of age before it starts producing acorns.

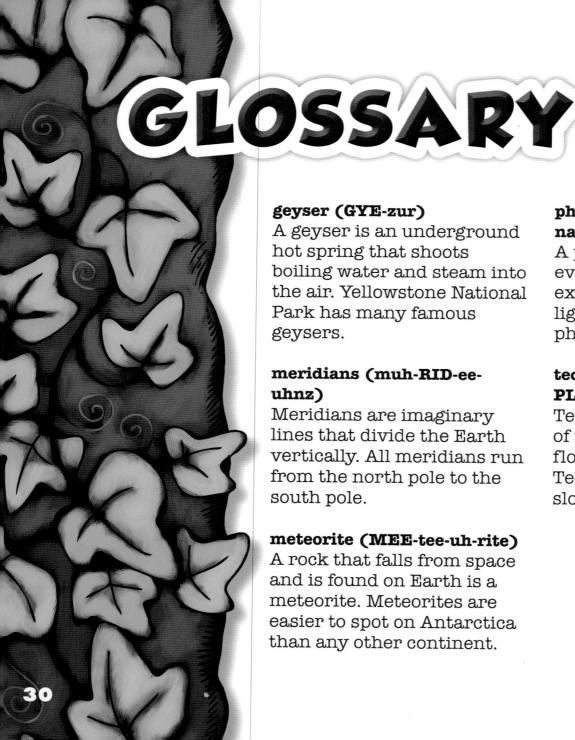

GLOSSARY

geyser (GYE-zur)
A geyser is an underground hot spring that shoots boiling water and steam into the air. Yellowstone National Park has many famous geysers.

meridians (muh-RID-ee-uhnz)
Meridians are imaginary lines that divide the Earth vertically. All meridians run from the north pole to the south pole.

meteorite (MEE-tee-uh-rite)
A rock that falls from space and is found on Earth is a meteorite. Meteorites are easier to spot on Antarctica than any other continent.

phenomenon (fuh-NAH-nuh-nahn)
A phenomenon is a fact or event that can be seen or experienced. The northern lights are an amazing phenomenon to witness.

tectonic plates (tek-TAH-nik PLAYTZ)
Tectonic plates are the layer of the Earth's crust that floats and moves around. Tectonic plates move very slowly.

LEARN MORE

BOOKS

Fradin, Judy and Dennis. *Volcanos.* Washington DC: National Geographic Society, 2007.

Glover, David. *Pocket Guides: Earth Facts.* New York: DK Publishing, 2004.

WEB SITES

Visit our Web site for links about weird Earth facts: **childsworld.com/links**

Note to Parents, Teachers, and Librarians: We routinely verify our Web links to make sure they are safe and active sites. So encourage your readers to check them out!

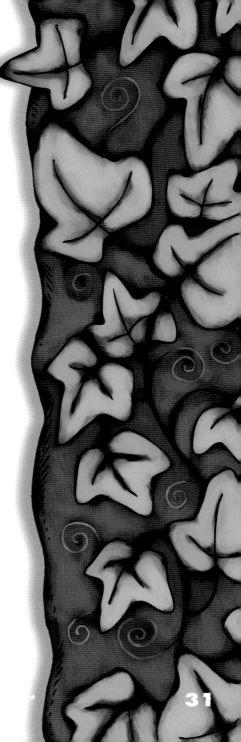

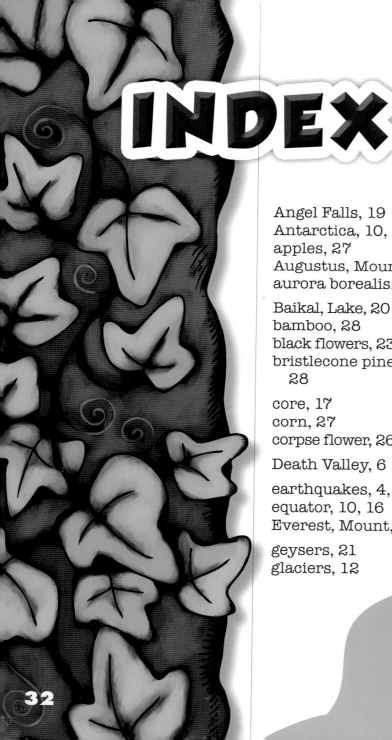

INDEX

WELCOME TO YELLOWSTONE